WINDOW TO THE WORLD; AM I JUST A WAITER?

WRITTEN BY: RANDELL (RB) BROWN

FROM THE EDITOR – SABRINA BLACK-HALL

In today's world, people are looking for instant gratification. There is no time to wait - for anything. We have the entire world at our fingertips, and yet - so many times we fail to interact with the world that is around us. We stare mindlessly at our phones, searching for something meaningful while we miss all the life that is around us.

This memoir is meant to serve as a reminder, a reminder to engage in the world around you. Appreciate the life that you have and all the people you encounter. It is not written in the traditional, chapter style. Instead, it is a collection of short summaries from the perspective of a waiter who encounters countless people on a daily, if not hourly basis, and how important he finds each encounter.

Rarely do people share a piece of themselves with people they know, let alone people that they have just met and will probably never see again. However, Randell would not be true to himself, or the memory of his mother, if he didn't share his version of the world with the people he encounters.

As you read this, please remember that these words are only the beginning, there are so many more memories left to share and lessons to pass on. While everyone has a mother, not everyone has a mom who inspires them to leave the world in a better way than they found it. As you read this, remember how important it is for Randell to pass on the light that his mother gave him, and take the time to pass the light onto someone else, so that we can all shine a little brighter.

DEDICATION:

Mom, I wrote this book for you. I wish you were here, in person, to share what's about to happen in my life. I thank you for teaching me about God and how important my relationship with him should be. You were right; you're not always going to be around.

I learned so much from you. I thank you for being my **#1 friend, #1 coach, #1 cheerleader,** and the **#1 real life person** that I could touch and share the most important developmental part of my life with. You helped to create the man I have become.

Since I lost you, I am more in tune with my mortality. I hear and see differently than ever before. I understand differently. I notice what most never do – what most obviously walk past – like a penny on the ground. **M.O.M**. I'm privileged to present to you:

WINDOW TO THE WORLD

INSPIRATION:

"The first responsibility of a leader is to define reality. The last is to say thank you. In between, the leader is a servant." – Max Depree

"Where there is no vision, the people perish." – Prv 29:18

"Before you are a leader, success is all about growing yourself. When you become a leader, success is all about growing others." – Jack Welch

PROLOGUE:

These **ruminations** are a collection of **songs, scripts, compliments, motivations, inspirations** and **blessings**. Read it not like a regular book, but rather a series of **short stories** about **experiences, events**, and **conversations.** As you read on, think about your life and what your **Window to the World** looks like.

What inspires you? What conversations will stay with you forever?

This book is a collage of passages, recollecting new experiences with new beautiful people: families, couples, friends, co-workers, etcetera. From the perspective of a waiter at an airport restaurant, I want to share my experiences with the people I meet and with whom I share mealtime - if only for once in their lives.

I like to call these encounters a **"table touch"**. Every time I meet a new table, I touch the table before I introduce myself. Imagine being served by a waiter at the busiest restaurant you've ever been to. Now, imagine how much is going on around you in that scenario.

WINDOW TO THE WORLD

Every day, I see and interact with more people than many do in a week and definitely more than I ever imagined I would. This is what I like to call my **Window to the World (WTTW)** Visualize the amount of people you see at a major rock concert, super bowl, a protest or demonstration, a popular mall in a big city. That's where I work.

My **WTTW** is geographically located at Dallas – Ft worth International Airport. Being a waiter in an environment where everyone is rushing, and has a flight to catch, the sentiment of time trumps leisure. Unless there is a delayed, canceled, or missed flight, time is of the essence. Compared to most restaurants outside of an airport environment, my job affords me an opportunity to interact with hundreds in a workday and see thousands of people a day.

There are so many beautiful people I wait on from all over the world, whom I help nurture for brief moments in their lives. **It is during these brief** moments we tend to miss or walk past the small things - like pennies on the ground.

AM I JUST A WAITER?

Script:

Waiter: Hello, I'm Randell. I'll be taking care of you. Welcome, and thank you for visiting Motivations of Many. May I get you started with a beverage? Maybe a '1-up', a **'M.O.M.'**, a 'There Moment', a 'Most Beautiful', or a 'What's the Dream'?

Guest: Uh, Uhhhh

Waiter: Did you need a little more time?

Guest: No, I'm ready. I'd like to start with a cup of **M.O.M.** and a glass of ice water, light ice.

Waiter: You've chosen a great cup of wisdom. Very popular thirst quencher, I'll get that request in for you. Would you like any starters or appetizers? Or would you like to look at the menu yourself?

Guest: I'll take a look for myself.

Waiter: Great, I'll be right back with your cup of **M.O.M.** and that water, light ice.

Guest: Thanks.

Waiter: My pleasure.

M.O.M.

Motivations of Many:

-**Mom,** I love you more than I could ever tell you.

-**Mom,** I love you more than I could ever show you.

-**Mom,** anything you've ever taught me in life that meant anything, we hear you. Sometimes we just don't hear it completely until we can't see you, talk to you, or touch you anymore.

-**Mom,** when it's the busiest time of day and the airport is jam packed around dinner time; I take this time to notice the most important thing in life, the people. The hundreds of thousands of people I've never seen before in my life. There are so many people in this world and we're all leaving one day.

-**Mom,** If I can physically touch a person that I am drawn to, intrigued by, or whom means something to me, my spirit will not allow me to obviously walk past. Ignoring these opportunities for meaningful interactions would be like walking over pennies – extremely foolish of me.

In this analogy, saying 'hello' to a beautiful person as I walk past them is synonymous with picking up an otherwise disregarded penny.

Living in the moment and not walking over pennies is all about, the people.

SONG: MY FAITH

If you've experienced
What I've experienced
Then you would know
Where I'm coming from
Chorus: My faith

>Has brought me this far

>Continue to use me God

>I wouldn't change a thing

>Including the hurt and the pain

Momma I made a vow
I promise to make you proud
Of me (2 times)

>Live in the moment and own it

>Like Momma always said

>Pay attention and focus

>Don't get distracted

>Momma, but the people be talkin'

>Sometimes I can hear them

>Momma, without you I'm lonely

>But forever I hear you

Some people gon throw salt on my game
Momma, when people be talkin'
All on my name
Sometimes I hear them
The things people say, the things people say

I'm going to tell them what you would tell me, to tell them
You don't even know me
You don't even know me
You don't even know me
You don't even know me

Chorus: My faith

>   Has brought me this far

>   Continue to use me God

>   I wouldn't change a thing

>   Including the hurt and the pain

NEBRASKA
A conversation

I was raised in Omaha, **Nebraska.** Working in this industry, I've found not many people know much about **Nebraska,** and therefore, I have made an effort to inform and connect with people about this tiny piece of me.

Pick up a penny.

Waiter: Where are you from?

Guest: All over.

Waiter: I've never been there; tell me something unique about where you're from.

For example:

1. Warren Buffet is from Nebraska
2. The Henry Doorly Zoo and Aquarium, one of the top-rated zoos in the country, is located in Omaha, NE.
3. Nebraska hosts the college world series every year
4. Malcom X was born in Omaha, NE
5. 911 George Bush III Offutt Air Force Base,

one of the most secure bases in the world, is in Nebraska.
6. Kool-Aid was invented in Hastings, NE
7. Vice grips were invented in Nebraska
8. Actress Gabrielle Union is from Nebraska
9. Johnny Carson is from Nebraska
10. The Huskers of course!

And in return, here are a few things that I've learned:

1. Pittsburg, PA has the most bridges in the country
2. Minneapolis, MN has the most skyways in the country
3. Whiffle ball was invented in Connecticut
4. Iowa produces the most corn in the country
5. Bourbon is only made in Kentucky
6. Tennessee has 2 of the best music recording technology programs located at the University of Memphis and Middle Tennessee state.
7. Louisiana has the tallest state capital, the longest bridge and parishes rather than counties
8. The frozen margarita machine was invented in Dallas, TX
9. New Mexico has the biggest hot air balloon festival in the country
10. Milwaukee, WI has the biggest

music festival in the country called Summerfest.

11. Fresno, CA produces the most grapes and pecans in the country.

12. Oregon is the home of Nike

13. Kansas is the aviation capital of the country

14. The film, "Shawshank Redemption" was filmed in Mansfield, OH

15. Sturgis, largest bike rally in the country, is located in South Dakota

Examining this interaction closely, you will see there is a trend - Pennies to people, people to pennies, we acquire knowledge through interaction. For this reason, the more valuable, personal interactions we have, the more knowledge we have. For this reason alone, I strive to go beyond just waiting tables; I'm creating an experience.

BLESSINGS: THE GLOW

Since losing my mother I see, hear, and feel differently than I had before. I'm more observant, conscious, and sensitive to the world.

The best way to explain The Glow is like this: after you see so many different people, so many different expressions – you realize that some of those faces and expressions just stand out. Some faces just don't fade into the sea of people, but light up the space around them? Well, that's the glow.

I have discovered 3 reasons people glow to me:

First: They have experienced a profound, life changing loss; the way I did when I lost my mother. There's a different level of loss when losing a **mom,** dad, brother, sister, child, spouse, grandparent.

Second: A person who experienced a life altering/ near-death experience. These are the survivors of any life experience meant for them to physically not survive and/or hinder them from' normal' life.

Third: Some people simply glow to inspire others.

The Glow has been validated to me in many ways and can be explained by this scenario:

One day at work, there was a woman in the restaurant having dinner with her son. Her back was to me, and without even seeing her face, I knew she had the glow, radiating from her.

After twenty minutes, I realized that if I didn't speak to this woman, I would never have another chance. When I approached her table, I immediately realized the source of her glow; she was pregnant. Even though I already felt it, it was nice to have that validation.

I can see the glow in people who are not pregnant as well. I use this gift and knowledge to engage and pass on blessings. If you stand out because of a shirt, hairstyle, smile, voice, action such as reading a book, etcetera. I make it a point to be present and validate the existence of this person who carries **This Glow.**

WHAT'S THE DREAM?

A conversation.

When I have the opportunity to engage a person college age or younger, I like to ask "What's your dream?"

We all have a divine right and purpose in our lives and it's important to reach our potential and destination.

To the world, there is only one true secret of attaining the dream.

The secret is to stay in the same room as the dream.

For example, if you want to play in the WNBA, NFL, MLB, NBA, etc.... If you don't make it to the league, you could still own a team, be the coach, be the personal trainer, or be the sports analyst.

You'll always be living the dream if you recognize the importance of staying in the same room.

One last example: My dream is to travel across the world, meet people, inspire them, and then send them on their way with a little piece of me.

Am I Just a Waiter?

NO! I'm a man of many titles: Author, Messenger, Singer, Songwriter, Man of God, Life Coach, Speaker, Waiter etc....

It's the small things we miss or walk past and never notice like a penny on the ground. I don't even have to travel. People come to me from all over the world one flight at a time. God is amazing...

No matter what title the world gives you, if you stay in the same room, you'll always be living the dream.

WHAT PROBLEM IN THE WORLD DO YOU WANT TO SOLVE?

A conversation

This is the new question to the world soon to replace

"What's your dream?" and "What do you want to be when you grow up?"

In such a disconnected society, with all the phones and selfies, we have to find unique ways of getting the children of the future to think of things that will have an effect on everyone, not just our own selfish dream. That's the genius of the question. "What problem in the world do you want to solve?" is a selfless question we need to start to train the future of our world to answer.

The problem I want to solve in the world is the disconnection of human interactions because of phones and social media. We're losing connection with the most important thing in life, the people. We are surrounded by people, the most important thing in life. Yet, some people believe their house is more important, or their car or bank account is more important than the people. **People have always been the secret to life.**

Sometimes we just don't fully understand until we lose a person close enough for us to wake up.

"Wake up world, there are billions of amazing people out there if you would just look up to notice".

DUMB DUMBS.
Think different

The destruction of the human connection has been caused by the dumb dumbs. The dumb dumbs can be better described and noticed as a phone. We'd rather talk to a phone than a real-life person. So simple and dumb we have become. The most important part about life is life itself, the people alive. People like You.

      Wake up world, we've become so selfish. The selfie is selfish because I wouldn't know that I meet more people than you if I was focused on my selfish Dumb Dumb....

We walk over people like pennies. 20/20 is vision. The Year "2020" is about vision as well, see the people. I claim that for the world.

Wake up world, there are billions of amazing people out there if you would just look up to notice".

INSPIRATION: WELCOME

The people of the world helped me heal. After my mother's passing, I moved back to Arkansas. I still remember the tree in front of the house on Flipper Street full of butterfly cocoons. **Was this a message?** Now, to notice **The Glow** of others that have lost, I give you a small blueprint to some of the ways our loved ones communicate with us all the time.

Through:

People, animals, **water,** nature, food, dreams, **butterflies,** blue birds, **red birds, clouds,** trees, flowers, **rain,** lights, **actions such as washing clothes,** rainbows, sunsets, wind, dragonflies, **moths,** coins, trains, **pennies,** etc.

Welcome is what I will forever say in someone's passing. We're so conditioned to say sorry. I'm more in tune with my inner spirit and what's going on around me than I've ever been. Others who have lost helped me understand and sharpen this growing gift.

Welcome

You will forever hear different, see different, become more sensitive to the world and you will notice things others don't notice such as a penny on the ground.

MOTIVATIONS OF MANY: THERE MOMENTS

> I wish my mother would be here.
> When I get married, she won't be.
> I wish my mother would be here.
> When I have kids, she won't be.

My mother was here for me during an important speaking engagement and now I can still feel her presence with me. I can feel her when I am speaking to the new people entering my life.

A **There Moment** happens when you are experiencing something, or someplace, for the first time. Everything you experience in that space belongs to you. This moment is yours to possess. You are the proud owner of this piece of time. Do what you will with it, but be there, in that moment.

Thanks **Mom,** for the **"There Moments"** you afforded me.

It's the small things we walk past and pay no never mind to that makes the most sense like a penny.

HOSPICE

Think different

Hospice and assisted care living are two of the sweetest ways to say goodbye in this life. It allows us to hear everything and say everything. My mom afforded us no regrets because of **hospice**. Thank you **M.O.M.**

Cure for Cancer dreamers and problem solvers?

Hospice is now my ally and I've grown to respect and appreciate it……

Hospice is what allowed me to understand, articulate, and create **"There Moments"**.

SCRIPT: AM I JUST A WAITER

Waiter: (Approaches table)

Guest: Hey, that **M.O.M.** was great. Nice selection.

Waiter: My pleasure. Were you ready to order or would you like some suggestions?

Guest: A few suggestions would be nice. I have a decent appetite and want something amazing.

Waiter: We have many items. I'll tell you about a few. First, it must begin with a 'Most Beautiful', one of our most popular items. We do carry a 'Front Street', it's very flavorful. "But if you love being woke…." then that **'Right On Time'** will change your life if you allow it to. This plate is accompanied with a side of perspective and most definitely some truth.

Guest: You sold me when you told me it would change my life. How so?

Waiter: Let's see.

BLESSINGS: RIGHT ON TIME

One thing I learned about time is that God's time is all that matters. Delays and cancellations are an unfortunate part of air travel. When I have a guest that's delayed, cancelled, on standby etc....

I tell them **"Everything you see, hear, taste, smell, touch, any person you interact with now, you would have never met or seen had you been on that flight. So, anything that was memorable would not have existed either. Pick up your pennies."**

When you make it to your destination, you will be **Right on Time.** This is then followed with, "Want me to tell you how I know?" And goes on to become me explaining

As humans, everything we do is regulated by time, from the moment we enter the world, until the moment we leave. How do we know where we are supposed to be? Time? How do we know when were supposed to be somewhere else? Time? But nobody knows how much time they have left. We all operate in a realm of unlimited minutes, but God does not. So, if you go by God's time, you will get there **right on time.**

My flight was cancelled when I was on my way back to Texas from spreading my mother's ashes in San Diego, California. **What I remember most was all the things we didn't have the time for because we were too preoccupied with everything we made the time for.** My siblings and I ate, danced, and I sang karaoke (Tom Petty's 'Free Falling') at the beach. Our mother was telling us to live and not focus on her passing, to never stop dancing (and to never date a girl that doesn't dance in the rain). She was telling us too simply

Pick up your pennies and notice the butterflies....

MOTIVATIONS OF MANY:

Most Beautiful

If I never see you again, **you are one of the most beautiful ladies I have ever met in my life.** I am privileged to not only admire your beauty, but to be able to tell you. You mean something to me and while I may never see you again, I'd like to acknowledge you've inspired me. You motivate me to be the best I can possibly be, and I want you to know that.

Most beautiful, never forget these words, You **Glow.** In the moment seeing you and meeting you, you're absolutely precious. For the rest of your life, that is what you are to the world. **It's the small things we overlook and walk past like a penny on the ground**.

I notice my pennies in people and make sense of life.

SONG: IF I NEVER SEE YOU AGAIN

If I never see you again
So amazing
Inspiration
I feel your presence
So bright, I can see the glow
You're one of the most beautifuls
That I will ever see in my life

I wish you were
I wish you were
I wish you were
Mine

Back to reality back to real world
So many beautifuls in the world
So much precious cargo
Look at her go
Look at her fly

My window to the world
The way that you walk
The way that you talk

The way that you do yeah
Everything that you do yeah

So much inspiration from you yeah
If I never see you again

CONVERSATION: FRONT STREET

Every now and again, I wait on a woman who says "that's the same line you ran on me before."

My response is always, "when you lose your #1 real life person in this world, **M.O.M,** it changes you". Meaning, **I will never walk past anything beautiful to me in this life; like a penny on the ground**.

If you stand out, glow. If I notice you again, it should only suggest "that you're consistent in your beauty".

So, that's really all it is. You're a constant glow to the universe. You are part of the inspiration that helped me finish this book for your information....

SCRIPT: JUST SAY THANK YOU

Waiter: Where are you from?

Guest: All over.

Waiter: You are one of the most beautiful ladies I have ever seen in my life.

Guest: How many girls do you say that to in a day?

Waiter: (Looks up, and then proceeds to lower his head back down towards the table) I don't know about your God, but my God is perfect, flawless, and amazing. It would be a shame if he only made one of you. Look up, all these people are just as important as you and guess what? They have a flight to catch too. There are so many beautiful people from different backgrounds and different ethnicities in many different shapes and many sizes.

Learn to **just say thank you...**

CONVERSATION: CAN'T SAY WHAT I SAY

This game is a great way to get groups involved, connected, thinking, and talking.

Tell me something most memorable about your trip?

Or, if they have yet to arrive,

What are you most looking forward to?

The catch, you can't repeat what has already been said.

The bigger the group, the more interesting this game becomes. It's always about the guests. **You're the ones traveling from all over the world. For a brief moment in life, we get to meet and share mealtime.** Therefore, it's important to make you feel at ease and comfortable in any way that I may be of service.

It's the small things we miss, walk past, pay no attention to, but because I notice now, my pennies

are beginning to make sense.

CIRCLES.
Think Different

How many people do you compliment, validate, show chivalry to or have a positive impact on, who are not in your **work circle, school circle, family circle, religious circle, or political circle?**

Every day I meet hundreds of people. I not only talk to people, I listen to them, share mealtime with them, and I get to see how well I listened by the correctness of the order. So intimate it is.

I get to see how amazing our creator is, more than most in the world, with God's greatest creation, PEOPLE.

Pennies to people.

SCRIPT: AM I JUST A WAITER

Waiter: How is everything?

Guest: Randell, you've made quite the impression. The meal is amazing.

Waiter: Did you leave room for a dessert? Maybe a "unique glow" a "two in one" or an "unexpected butterfly".

Guest: That unexpected butterfly sounds delicious. I'll have one.

Waiter: One unexpected butterfly coming up.

MOTIVATIONS OF MANY: THE BUTTERFLY

When you lose, you win. What have you won? If you haven't lost big, you someday will. That's what I won.

When my Mother passed, it sent me to her home back in Arkansas, good ol' Flipper Street. In the front yard there was a tree. The weekend of my mother's funeral, on this tree I saw hundreds of butterfly cocoons. I had to tap the nearest person to me, my nephew Micah. I asked him, "Do you see this? No one else will ever believe me." He told me he saw the cocoons.

Butterflies are what awakened me to the sensitivities I now have to the world. Butterflies are also one of the ways my mother was able to teach me two more life lessons.

Second to last Lesson – We're All Dying

"Son, for the rest of your life, every person you know and everyone you meet and see are all dying. Everyone is dying sooner than they think, including you Randell. Never stop dancing and being about the people. Follow your dreams. **People are the secret to life. "Take care of the people and the people will take care of you."**

FINAL LESSON - HOW TO DIE.

My **M.O.M.** Verdell Baker literally sang **"I Won't Complain"** the last day we were together. I'll remember that forever **M.O.M.**, I embrace you and thank you for my final lesson in this world.

Metamorphosis: A true loss alters a person's meaning of life and everything they perceive as true and logical changes. Metamorphosis is what butterflies do. They go through an extensive process of complete transformation. My **M.O.M.** speaks to me through the butterflies.

INSPIRATION: 1-UP

My mother always told me to praise God and love the woman who truly loves all of me. She told me once I found this woman to live life, follow my dreams, be happy, and then, be done.

Twenty to thirty times a day I see the most beautiful women I will ever see in my life. The most gorgeous women you could ever imagine I encounter every day.

What I've learned is:

There are always prettier eyes.

There is always a more beautiful smile.

There is always more amazing hair.

There are always bigger tatas.

There is always a just right derriere.

I realized that I only need one woman. We only get one **M.O.M.** Fellas, when it's time to settle down, don't get caught up in the 1-up thinking that she has a little bit more than the last. Focus, men and women. If you're already looking, you're already losing. Focus on what you have now. Wake up. **Stop to notice and appreciate the small things you already have in each other, unlike the pennies you both walk over. Issues that arise in a partnership or relationship often tend to be reminiscent of the quote**

"Don't make no cents and you wonder why the relationship is broke". R.B.

SONG: REPERCUSSIONS

Talk the way you talk
Live the way you live
Play the way you play
But understand one thang
You must face the repercussion
See, back in the day, man
Amen that I wasn't consumed, by something
That was supposed to consume
My life for ruins
Nights alone
Yes
Many fears many tears
I didn't know what to expect
Next
Transition from being at home
To another place

Is this gon be what it is
Is this gon be how I live
I pray for my love to give
Me another chance
See the repercussions I
Was facin'
Wasn't no gettin' away from
I had to gon and face it

Talk the way you talk

RANDELL BROWN

Live the way you live
Play the way you play
But understand one thang
You must face the repercussion

Talk the way you talk
Live the way you live
Play the way you play
But understand one thang
You must face the repercussion

CONVERSATION: EXHALE

Whenever I'm working and see a sista' at the bar, I scan the restaurant to see if she's the only one. It may come as a surprise to some, but at the airport, the predominant population tends to be the other - not the brotha or sista.

If she is in fact the only one, I walk up to her and ask: "Remember the movie **'Waiting to Exhale?'** Remember the scene with Angela Bassett at the bar - then Wesley Snipes enters and says. **'You've got to be an amazing and strong sista to be the only one at this bar.'** "

The Sista' slightly pauses as she revisits the movie in her mind. She giggles shyly, and says, "You're so silly". I tell her, "You did that"

My brothas and I have a similar interaction. When I see you, we discuss the stereotypes and stigmas some people have placed on us blacks, followed by conversations, outlining change. I explain to the brothas I encounter that not everyone gets these types of opportunities; they've been blessed to have the access to travel. **Pennies also stand for patience.**

CONVERSATION: LOVE LANGUAGE

When you encounter thousands of people a day, it becomes easy to be drawn to people who are genuinely happy and couples that are in love. Sometimes I see couples whose energy is so bright. It's rather difficult not to see love if it exists. When love stops in the restaurant and visits me, this is the first thing I say.

Waiter: There are five love languages.

    Words of affirmation

    Quality time

    Acts of kindness

    Personal touch

    Receiving Gifts

Y'all are so in love, it illuminates the room. I want my love to look like yours. If people watch you, it's because you glow. They look at their life, then look at yours and wonder; why doesn't my life glow like yours?

SCRIPT: AM I JUST A WAITER

Waiter: Did y'all want another round, or were y'all ready to tab out?

Guest: We'll take the tab, everything was great.

Waiter: Here you go; I already had your tab ready. I'll be your cashier when you're ready.

Guest: Thanks, here you are. We can settle with you now.

Waiter: It was a pleasure meeting you. I've never met you before in my life, and that's the privilege. **It's the small things we miss and walk past like a penny on the ground.**

Guest: We'll always remember you Randell. Be blessed. May your dreams come true. Here you go; you can keep the change.

Waiter: Thanks enjoy your flight.

SONG: LOSE TO WIN

Sometimes the sun won't shine
And sometimes it, rains
Tell me how it makes you feel
Tell me about the pain
How it never seems to end
Corners we bend

When we ride on the block
Hold on to stay in the lane
No more living in the past
No more living with regrets

If you're amazing
I'll tell you
If you're beautiful
I'll tell you

Live in the moment and own it
Live in the moment and own it

WINDOW TO THE WORLD

Sometimes ya gotta lose to win
Sometimes ya gotta lose to win

Live in the moment and own it
Live in the moment and own it
Sometimes ya gotta lose to win
Sometimes ya gotta lose to win

INSPIRATION: MY BAD

Mistakes are inevitable and I apologize for mine. I like to blame it on my head, not my heart. In the restaurant industry, we are not always on the ball; sometimes it's the kitchen staff preparing the food, the host seating you, the busser cleaning the table. Sometimes it's **you.**

Just be nice to people.

EXPERIENCE: I HOPE YOU LOSE YOUR LUGGAGE

The following should not be funny, but it is. We are all people. Therefore, we should all take care of other people better than we do. Not everyone deals with abuse the same. **Abuse to us in the service industry can include: horrible tips, rude guests, belligerently needy and or picky people, thinking you are the only one needing something, exhibiting societal privilege, and general inconsideration of the staff and others around you.**

A buddy of mine told a group that was rude and didn't tip,

"I hope you lose your luggage."

WOW.

Because I believe karma catches us all, I only had

one piece of advice to my coworker. Just be nice to people especially if you know that you'll never see each other again in this life.

EXPERIENCE: SOME PEOPLE (CAN'T MAKE EVERYONE HAPPY)

I should title this **"The Customer Isn't Always Right."** Who came up with that other saying? People are people and we all are fallible. You do order the wrong drink, entrée, or misread something on the menu. Yes, you do, we all do. I've done it myself.

Making an honest mistake is one of the few things that bring us back to the realization that we are one thing, simply; **we are humans living human experiences.**

Waiter: My apologies. Can I make this right for you?
Guest: Oh, no. You're out of time now.
Waiter: Is there anything I can do?

Guest: Ya, you could have gotten my drink order right the first time.
Waiter: (Quietly walks away from table)

Speak to people with respect. Treat people how you would want your **M.O.M.** to be treated. In the above scenario, if I responded with the same rudeness as the guest, it would've cost me my job. I must emotionlessly take your insults, shake them off, and focus on the next table. Because, truth is, I may never see you again in my life. So, would it be worth it?

I WILL DIE FOR YOU

Think different

I meet hundreds of people on a daily basis which means I have the validity to tell you about the most amazing humans alive today.

First and foremost, that accolade is dedicated to the men and women of the armed forces and any type of first responder. **You're most amazing because you sign on the dotted line with your life for so many people who underestimate your sacrifice.**

Furthermore, anyone that is a servant to people through interaction.

TSA, airport gate agents, Mary Kay, teachers, doctors, nurses, hairstylists, beauticians, tattoo artist, dentists, trainers of any type, fast food employees, Walmart employees, servers, bartenders, etc.

You're so amazing because you regularly get treated badly and, yet, you still have to take care of people. These interactions provide a blueprint and opens your eyes to truly understand and believe that there are more amazing people than people you couldn't care less to ever have known....

Inspiration: "You walk for the fallen"

I appreciate you. Every day I get to meet and see thousands of people from all over the world. People travel without worry because of you. You're selfless and I appreciate you.

I can recall a time when a guest offered to pay for a serviceman's tab. The woman noticed him in uniform immediately as he walked into the restaurant. I went on to let the woman know how much I appreciated her for the gesture toward the serviceman. She proceeded to tell me that she lost her son In Iraq; the uniform allowed her son to spiritually visit in that moment.

My mother worked at Mary Kay cosmetics since before I was born. This has likely contributed to it being so easy for me to talk to people. Each year, the annual Mary Kay Convention is held in Dallas, Texas. Working at DFW Airport, I can always tell Mary Kay Convention time because my mother visits me through the many men and women representing Mary Kay; through bumble bees, shades of pink, the polished flair, flawless make-up, limitless energy, etc.

Please know that whenever you are in uniform and around hundreds of people. Though you may never know, you walk for the fallen. I appreciate this penny in you that isn't noticed nearly enough.

COMPLIMENT: TWO IN ONE

Think about a time when you've seen two absolutely gorgeous people. Knowing that you may never see them again, what's your next move? In situations like these, I stop and acknowledge a person's beauty. I simply stop, and I tell them.

Waiter: Excuse me ladies. I see so many people I may never see again. I call these encounters my **"Window to the World"** and now you're a part of that. Thank you for stopping in, because if you hadn't, I would only be afforded to notice you until you were gone, possibly forever. You're both beautiful, and in this moment, so many other people would just watch you or choose to talk to one of you. Shame on them, I choose both of you because this message isn't for me. It's for you. If I never see you again, it'd be selfish to go by without telling you, you stand out.

COMPLIMENT: SO SEASONED, BEAUTY IS LONGEVITY

Over the years of seeing so many people, my views of beautiful have been renewed.

Beautiful to me now is when she has a book in her possession.
Beautiful now is when her back is turned against everyone because she isn't concerned about being the center of attention.
Beautiful now is when she isn't constantly on the phone and taking selfies.
Beautiful now is when she expresses her style and uniqueness with her clothes on.
Beautiful now is the seasoned ladies that have had children, grandchildren, great grandchildren, experienced loss and she's still beautiful. WOW.

Not all people in their 20's and 30's will make it to be seasoned but these 20 and 30-year olds walk around as if the entire world revolves around their beauty.

My advice to these individuals is; give it time, your high school reunion will tell who smoked too much, drank too much, experimented with too many drugs, stayed in the sun too long, or just had a hard life. Longevity is essential. This led me to believe that the most beautiful people are those whom are seasoned or have aged gracefully. We must understand that longevity requires being chosen for purpose. Being seasoned is synonymous with being classic, ageless or with a childlike presence.

MOTIVATIONS OF MANY: I APPRECIATE YOU

If you are a survivor of anything that was meant to halt or disrupt your normal daily life, **I appreciate you.** To those that don't walk the same, look the same, and/or behave the same as the status quo - **I appreciate you.** To those with wheelchairs, missing limbs, or any exterior differences that make you unique - **I appreciate you.** You walk for the people like you who refuse to leave their home or the confines of their community because of what so many 'able bodied' people have to say. You're extraordinary for the walk that you take every day.

    I appreciate you because you see life in a way that many will never understand. I've learned in life; every single human has a scar. However, sometimes if our scars aren't as visible as others, we whisper, laugh, heckle and joke about others who may not be the same as us. I call you extraordinary because it takes a special human being to carry this glow.

But that's why they notice you.

They only pay attention because you glow.

MOTIVATIONS OF MANY: PENNIES FROM HEAVEN

One day, I met a woman who told me a story about **pennies**. In short, she began to collect **pennies** after her parents, who collected **pennies** throughout their lives, passed away. She theorized that every **penny** that caught her eye represented her parents' spirits attempting to communicate with her.

Since meeting her, I met someone else, who mentioned that the song, "**Pennies** from Heaven" was played at her mother's funeral.

<u>**"Welcome**, you will forever hear different, see different, become more sensitive to the world than you've ever become, and you'll sometimes notice things that others don't notice such as a **penny** on the ground".</u>   RB

This is how the story of the **penny** began for

me. I once dropped a **penny** in the middle of the airport terminal on a busy day. Watching it, I noticed that the only way the **penny** moved was if it was walked over or kicked. It's the small things we miss. While some people pick up **pennies,** some collect them, some turn them to the lucky side heads up, most of us simply walk over them. Again, it's the little things we miss in life.

The penny is the absolute sum of everything in this world and we spend them every day.

Most of us want thousands or even millions of dollars and everything in this world that money can buy. Yet, most people walk over the sum of absolutely everything and believe that they have it all together.

Pennies represent compliments that we walk past because were too self-absorbed to receive the love of others. **Pennies represent chivalry** but the first person on the plane is not interested in the last person on the plane - be patient. **Pennies represent all the basic life functions** that people take for granted every day. Talk, touch, taste, smell, hear, see, breath; we expect what is a gift then we walk right over a **penny.**

Only until it truly makes sense will the penny be valued. I notice what other people don't notice now and it took me losing to actually win.

Now, whenever a penny is on the floor in the restaurant. I look for a **M.O.M.** or family to share the story of a penny. **It's the small things we miss and walk past like a penny on the ground.**

SCRIPT: AM I JUST A WAITER

Waiter: To all the beautiful, amazing people I met. I thank you for your blessings, motivations, thank you for loving me. Each one of you inspired me to complete this work. Please know that.

Thank you, Lord for you have allowed me the opportunity to meet so many amazing, beautiful people and be a messenger of your word in a transparent context. I'll never forget about the people.

"Take care of the people, and the people will take care of you".

"Randell, you're doing great things. Stay focused on your career, keep moving forward, and the rest will follow with great success"

-Mom-

ABOUT THE AUTHOR

Randell Brown is an author, speaker, and musician from Dallas, TX. He is one of five children and has a twin sister. He is an accomplished speaker who has won toastmasters speaking competitions. Mr. Brown's speaking engagements include local schools, Texas Christian University, Volunteers of America, The University of Arkansas Pine Bluff, and The University of Texas at Arlington, to name a few.

Made in the USA
Columbia, SC
21 November 2022